DISCLAIMER

This book is a BASIC guide only. It serves as an introduction to car maintenance. It will explain terms and help you understand what is under the bonnet of your car. It will enable you to ask more intelligent questions when you meet with your mechanic. This book is not meant to be a replacement for professional advice. ALWAYS seek the assistance of a qualified professional before proceeding. In no event will the author be liable to you or anyone else for any loss or damage resulting from reliance on the information in this book or for any consequential loss or damage.

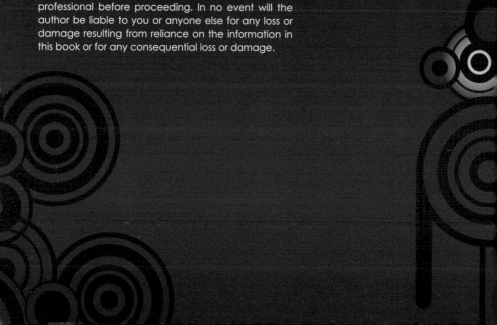

The essential guide to...

Car Care
for girls

Everything a girl needs to know about
taking care of her car

Danielle McCormick

Published by RTB Media
RTB Media Ltd Registered Offices:
7 Vernon Court, Clontarf, Dublin 3
www.rtbmedia.ie

Printed by DC Kavanagh Ebrook, Dublin

ISBN (978-0-9557329-0-4)

With thanks to the following for their kind contributions:
Denise Kinsella for being amazing and not taking
second best as an option. Louise Daly for photography.
Susan Meaney for design. Judith Schweppe for her kind
contribution. Elizabeth Dempsey for being pretty and
patient. David Fox for being foxy. Andrew for being
king of the castle. Dermott Lee for knowing all about
cars. Lorna for lending us her Barbie car and to Noelle
Moran for teaching me everything she knows about
books. And finally, a special thanks to my parents.

Contents

Section 1
HOW YOUR CAR WORKS

Who says that boys have to know more about cars than girls? Believe it or not, understanding and looking after your car isn't as hard as you think it is. Like most things in life, it is really easy when you know how! That's why we've put together this handy little book to tell you everything you need to know about how your car works and guide you through what to do when things go wrong. We have tried to break down the jargon and present all the info you need in a way that is sexy, fun and above all, easy for us girls to get our heads around.

The Essential Guide to Car Care for Girls is split into 4 sections: How Your Car Works, Car Maintenance, When Things Go Wrong and the Car Doctor. You can pick this book up and dip into individual sections as you need them or you can read it from cover to cover – it's up to you. You might want to become a mechanical expert so that you can talk the talk next time you have to face your mechanic. Equally the mechanics of your car might be as exciting as doing a tax exam but you could find the maintenance section really helpful to learn what checks you are supposed to be doing to keep your wheels in tip top shape. So whether you girls want to brush up on your mechanical lingo, impress the boys with your car knowledge or simply change a tyre without breaking a nail – this is the book for you!!

LET'S GET STARTED...

When the automobile was first invented there was such excitement about this amazing piece of machinery that could transport people long distances in great comfort. However now cars have become such an ingrained part of our everyday life we take them completely for granted. When you are sitting in your car you are sitting in a highly sophisticated piece of machinery with probably no clue as to how anything inside it works!

We tend to care more about things when we understand them, so hopefully when you appreciate how all the different parts of your car are working for you, you will return the favour and give your car the on-going TLC it deserves.

There are thousands of different makes and models of cars on our roads today. The majority of modern cars are all based around the same type of engine but each model will have slight variations on how all the components work together compared to another model. In order to best explain to you how your car works we are going to explain to you here how a "typical" engine works.

From the time you turn your key in the ignition to the moment when your wheels actually start turning there are lots of different processes happening at great speed. Before we go through a run through of the process from start to finish, there is one place that is worth looking at in more detail because this is where all the action takes place – **the cylinders.**

Some wonderful scientists discovered that if you add a tiny amount of high energy fuel (such as petrol) to a larger volume of air (roughly 1 part of petrol to 14 parts air) you can create a very useful gas. When this gas is put in a small enclosed space and ignited, it releases an incredible amount of energy. Then some exceptionally clever scientists discovered that they could use this energy in a useful way to get machines to carry us around. The next thing you know the noble horse was out of a job and the automobile came into being.

THE MAIN COMPONENTS YOU NEED TO UNDERSTAND INSIDE THE CYLINDER ARE:

1. **The piston** – a sliding piece of metal that moves up and down inside the cylinder.

2. **The intake valve** – the part of the cylinder that allows the air/fuel mix inside the chamber.

3. **The exhaust valve** – the part of the cylinder that releases the exhaust (used) fumes from the chamber.

4. **Internal combustion chamber** – When the pistons move down the cylinder they create an enclosed space which contains the explosions made by the ignited fuel.

5. **The spark plug** – The part which produces the spark which ignites the air/fuel mix.

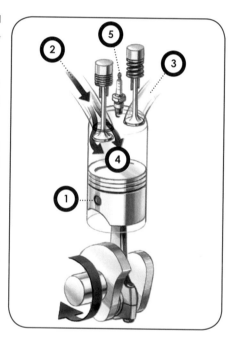

Almost all of today's modern car engines use what is known as a **four-stroke-combustion-cycle** to create movement. To put it in simpler terms, there are four movements which happen in a particular order that consume fuel and result in the release of a useful energy.

FOUR STROKE COMBUSTION CYCLE

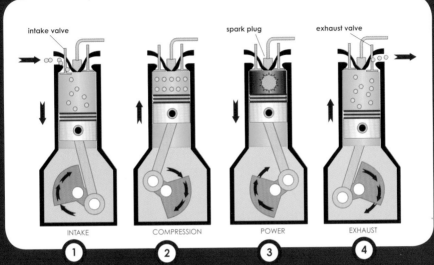

intake valve   spark plug   exhaust valve

INTAKE   COMPRESSION   POWER   EXHAUST

1   2   3   4

1. The first stroke is known as the **intake stroke**: The cycle begins with the piston at the top of the cylinder. The intake valve opens and the piston moves down the cylinder allowing the air/fuel mix to enter the open space.

2. Next is the **compression stroke**: The piston now moves back up towards the top of the cylinder thereby squeezing the air/fuel mix into a smaller space (i.e. compression). This will ultimately make the explosion more powerful.

3. When the piston has reached the highest point up in the cylinder that it can go, the spark plug emits a spark which ignites the air/fuel mix causing an explosion. The force of this explosion forces the piston back down the cylinder with great force. The bottom of the pistons are attached at right angles to a long cylindrical bar called a **crankshaft**. The up and down motion of the pistons in this cycle rotate the crankshaft in a similar way to the up and down motion of your legs on a bicycle. Ultimately, the motion that comes out of the engine is rotational which, funnily enough is exactly the motion needed to turn the wheels of a car! This rotational force is known as **torque.**

4. Finally, after the explosion, the exhaust valve opens and the piston moves back up to the top of the cylinder forcing the exhaust fumes out of the exhaust valve. Now that it is at the top of the cylinder it is ready to start the cycle again.

REVOLUTIONS PER MINUTE

In a car engine this cycle repeats itself inside each cylinder thousands of times a minute. This is where the expression "Revs (or revolutions) per minute" comes from. Your **rev counter** is telling you how many thousand times per minute these explosions are occurring in your cylinders. Next time you are driving check out your rev counter and see how hard your engine is working for you!

CYLINDER BANKS

V-shaped cylinder bank

There are a number of cylinders in your engine. The number you have depends on what type of car you have. The cylinders can be arranged in a number of different shapes e.g. in-line means they are arranged in a row; "v" means they are arranged in two banks (rows) in a "v" shape; "flat" means there are two opposing banks but in a flat shape. When someone says they have a "v6" or "v8" engine, it means there are 6 or 8 cylinders arranged in a V shape.

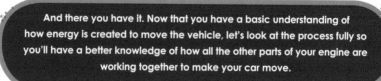

And there you have it. Now that you have a basic understanding of how energy is created to move the vehicle, let's look at the process fully so you'll have a better knowledge of how all the other parts of your engine are working together to make your car move.

WHAT HAPPENS WHEN I TURN THE KEY IN THE IGNITION?

When you turn the key in the ignition the **battery** powers the **starter motor** which begins to turn the crankshaft to get the pistons moving.

Air then enters your engine via a filter which removes any dirt or grit from the incoming air. At this point fuel (either petrol or diesel) is added to the air to create a vapourised gas. This gas is now waiting in a chamber for you to decide how much of it goes into the engine. The amount of this gas which goes into your engine is controlled by your foot on the accelerator pedal. If you want to add more fuel to your engine (to go fast or climb a hill) you must press the accelerator pedal down as much as it can go. This opens the valves wide allowing large amounts of gas through. If you only need a little bit of power (and therefore fuel) you only put your foot down lightly on the pedal which will only open the valve a fraction.

From here the gas goes through what is called an **intake manifold** which essentially distributes the gas through a series of passages to each of the cylinders. The opening and closing of these valves is carried out by the **camshaft.**

In most cars, when air enters the engine (to be mixed with fuel) the way it comes in is the way it is used. In some cars however, the air is pressurised (so more air/fuel mix can be squeezed into the cylinder) to increase performance. This is referred to as **turbo-charged** or **turbo-boost.**

NOW WE COME TO THE CYLINDER BIT

The gas then enters each cylinder via the **intake valve**. The piston comes up to the top of the cylinder and at this point the valves are closed.

> **The explosions that occur inside the different cylinders are timed to go off at different intervals ensuring the crankshaft is continually being spun.**

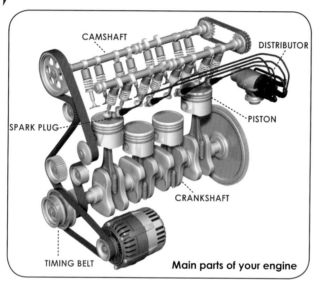

CAMSHAFT
DISTRIBUTOR
PISTON
SPARK PLUG
CRANKSHAFT
TIMING BELT

Main parts of your engine

At the exact same time the **distributor** causes a spark to go to the **spark plug** which ignites the fuel in the cylinder causing an explosion. The force of the explosion pushes the piston down the cylinder sharply. The pistons are attached at a right angle to the **crankshaft**. As the piston is forced down it causes the crankshaft to rotate.

So now your pistons are making the crankshaft rotate rapidly. Before all this motion goes to your wheels you need to be able to control it (so your car doesn't go 100 miles an hour when you only need to go 30!), therefore, the crankshaft goes through a section called the **transmission**. This section of the car is in charge of controlling the power contained in the crankshaft before it goes to the wheels.

The transmission controls the speed/power of your car by providing you with different speed/power ratios otherwise known as gears. For example, in first gear you need a lot of power to initially get your car moving, but you don't need a lot of speed. In a higher gear, the same amount of power would get you a higher speed. The transmission is responsible for regulating all of this. If you have a manual car, you manually control it with your gear stick.

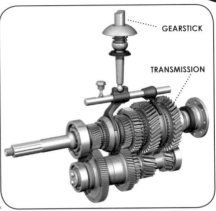

The crankshaft is not permanently connected to the transmission. You connect it to the transmission when you engage the clutch. This is why when you have your car in neutral, your engine is running but the wheels don't turn.

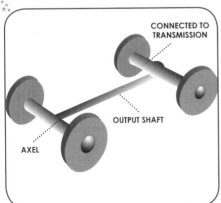

The transmission is connected to the **output shaft** which is connected to **axels** which are in turn connected to the wheels. When the transmission turns the output shaft; this turns the axels which in turn rotates your wheels. Et voila – You're moving!

Now you know how all the main components are working to make your car move it's time to look at the other vital components.

ELECTRONIC CONTROL UNIT (ECU)

In recent years cars have become much more high-tech and now even have computers in them programming certain elements of your engine. The Electronic Control Unit controls lots of things such as the fuel injection system, air-conditioning, air-flow and idle speeds (i.e. when you are sitting in traffic). In some instances, when you bring your car to your mechanic or dealership they will be able to plug a laptop into your car and get readings of how all the different components attached to the system are working.

> The ECU is also sometimes referred to as "the brains".

OIL

There are a lots of moving parts in your engine and oil makes sure that all parts are lubricated so they can move easily.

The main parts that need oil are:

1. **The pistons** – so they can slide up and down the cylinders.

2. **The camshaft and the crankshaft** – they have bearings which enable them to move freely and oil is used on these bearings to help them move.

Usually oil is sucked out of the oil pan by a pump which then passes it through a filter to remove any dirt. The oil is then squirted under high pressure onto the bearings and the cylinder walls. The oil then trickles down into an area called **the sump,** where it is collected. The process then starts all over again.

THE ALTERNATOR

The alternator is an important player in the electrical system of your car.

When the battery has started your car engine there is a belt within your engine that begins to rotate. The movement of this belt creates mechanical energy which the alternator then converts to electrical energy. This is not unlike the way the rotational movement of a windmill creates electrical energy. This energy goes to the alternator which then feeds this energy into the battery. The alternator provides the electricity which sparks the spark plug which then powers the cylinders.

Alternator

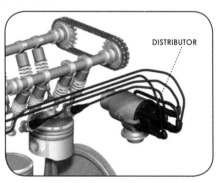
DISTRIBUTOR

THE REGULATOR

This is a device which regulates the amount of energy in the alternator to ensure it has just the right amount of energy it needs.

THE DISTRIBUTOR

The distributor gets the **ignition coil** to generate a spark at the precise instant that it is needed. It is also responsible for directing (i.e. distributing) that spark to the right cylinder at the right time. It has to do this at exactly the right instant and up to several thousand times a minute for each cylinder in the engine. If the timing spark is off by even a fraction of a second the engine will run poorly or not at all.

A misfiring spark plug can reduce fuel efficiency by as much as 30%

TIMING BELT

The camshaft (at the top of the cylinder) and crankshaft (at the bottom of the cylinder) need to work in synchronisation. The timing belt is a belt which is connected between the two, ensuring that they work in time with each other.

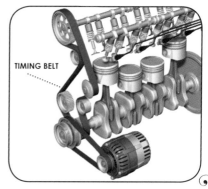

 Consult your **owner's manual** to find out how often your timing belt needs to be changed.

Depending on the model of your car, timing belts usually need to be replaced every 60,000 -100,000 miles.

CAR RADIATOR

THE COOLING SYSTEM

With all the fuel being burnt, as you can imagine, the engine will get quite hot! As a result, your car has a cooling system which keeps the temperature of the engine down. The cooling system mainly consists of the **radiator** and **water pump**. Water circulates through passages around the cylinders and then travels through the radiators to cool down.

EXHAUST SYSTEM

Remember when the gas was burned in the combustion chamber? As soon as it has been burnt it exits the combustion chamber via an **exhaust valve** and enters an exhaust system.

Most modern cars have a **catalytic converter** in their exhaust system which burns off any unused fuel and certain chemicals before it is released from the car via the **exhaust pipe**. The catalytic converter minimises the amount of toxic fumes coming from your car.

HEAD GASKET

The **head gasket** is tucked away inside your engine so it's not something that you see when you open up your bonnet but if it blows you can expect a big bill from your mechanic!

WHAT IS IT AND WHY DO I NEED TO WORRY?

The **cylinder head** (the block that seals all the tops of your cylinders) is made in one part of the car factory and the **engine block** (which contains all the main bodies of the cylinders) is made in another part of the factory. When it comes to putting your engine together these two pieces need to fit seamlessly together. With all the explosions taking place inside the cylinders there is no room for cracks or open spaces! So, in order to ensure the cylinder head and engine block fit seamlessly together the car people put a piece of metal called a head gasket in between them.

If your engine overheats for a sustained amount of time the head gasket can warp or crack and eventually blow. Replacing a head gasket is very labour intensive and therefore very costly. That is why it is really important that as soon as your engine shows any sign of overheating, pull over as soon as it is safe to do so and call for roadside assistance. It is generally much cheaper to call for roadside assistance than to replace a head gasket.

Keeping a constant check on your oil and coolant levels will help prevent these situations from happening. This is why our Dads/boyfriends/ brothers keep nagging us to do these seemingly unimportant little things. Now we know why there is actually a good reason we should listen to them!

BRAKES

There are usually two different types of brakes in your car; **disc brakes** and **drum brakes**. Disc brakes work in a very similar way to the brakes on a bicycle. On a bicycle there is a piece called a **caliper** which squeezes the brake pads against the wheel. In a car the disc brakes has a caliper (guarded with brake pads) which grabs onto the **rotor** of the wheel to get them to stop. Drum brakes work on the same principles as disc brakes. However, a drum brake presses against the inside of the wheel.

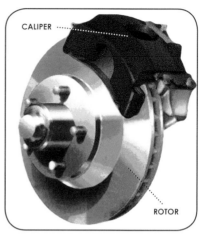

Typical disc brake system

The force that is used to get the brake pads to work is transmitted hydraulically i.e. through a fluid. When you step on your brake pedal you are actually pushing against a plunger which forces brake fluid through a series of tubes and hoses which ultimately puts pressure on the brake pads to stop your wheels.

A drop in brake fluid will affect the pressure in the system and therefore your braking capability. If you notice a drop in your brake fluid level (see **Brake Fluid** in Car Maintenance section) immediately consult your mechanic.

The brake pads wear down over time and need to be replaced quite regularly. If you hear noises when your car is braking it's time to bring it to your mechanic!

So that's it. Now you should be able to wow the boys with your knowledge of cars! Aren't you clever?!

Now that you know what all the different parts of your engine do let's see where they are when you open your bonnet. Not all car engines are the same so be aware that the parts of your engine might be arranged slightly differently.

1) INTAKE MANIFOLD

2) CYLINDERS

3) ELECTRONIC COMPUTER USAGE

4) SPARK PLUGS

5) RADIATOR

6) BATTERY

Section 2
CAR MAINTENANCE

It is more than likely that your car is one of the most expensive purchases you will ever make, so doesn't it make sense to look after it properly?

If you don't look after your car you can expect more expensive trips to the mechanic (and it's usually when you can least afford it!) and you'll probably get a lower re-sale value on your car.

Basic car maintenance is actually quite simple when you know how. Get into the habit of setting aside a few minutes every fortnight or so and carry out the basic checks in this section.

Before we begin...
OWNER'S MANUAL

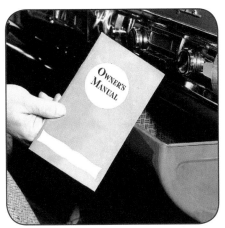

Doesn't it sometimes feel like the owner's manual was written by 'boys' for 'boys'? There are lots of technical words and not a lot of pretty pictures! But don't try and avoid it; your owner's manual is an essential tool to running and maintaining your car. You are not expected to read the manual cover to cover, just refer to the sections you need to when you need them. You may even find that when you do start reading the section on for example, oil, that it is surprisingly easy to understand.

Make sure you keep the owner's manual in a safe place in your car. It is usually designed to fit neatly into your glove compartment, so try and keep it there! It should give you such basic information from how to open your bonnet to how to change your tyre. Just look up the index on the section you need to get the page reference. Then go to the page to find out what you need to know.

If your car has lost its owner's manual, try and get another one for your car's precise make and model. You can get them from your car dealer and many are now available to order online.

SYMBOLS ON YOUR DASHBOARD

Cars are becoming much more sophisticated and in newer cars there tends to be a lot more sensors in various parts relaying information to your dashboard to notify you if something isn't right. You should familiarise yourself with the meaning of your dashboard symbols by consulting your owner's manual. Older cars won't be as good at telling you if something is wrong, so you really have to look after them carefully!

> **An orange symbol usually means you have a problem and should probably get it checked at your earliest convenience. A red symbol means you should stop using your car and get it checked by a mechanic immediately.**

HERE ARE SOME EXAMPLES OF COMMON SYMBOLS:

 Engine warning: Depending on your make of car this usually means there is a problem somewhere in your engine's management system.

 Oil: If this light shows, check your oil levels immediately. A lack of oil can lead to over-heating which can seriously damage your engine.

 Battery: If this light shows it means you are experiencing problems with your battery. It can be one of a number of things:
• Your battery's terminals may need cleaning
• It is not being charged properly by the alternator
• Your battery usually has a life of 3.5 years so may be nearing the end of its life and needs replacing.

 Brakes: This indicates that you have a problem somewhere in your brake system. You can check your brake fluids to see if they are low but generally all matters that relate to your brake system should be left to the professionals, so bring your car to a mechanic as soon as possible.

 Engine Over-heating: This symbol means your engine is over-heating. Pull over as soon as it is safe to do so and call for roadside assistance.

 ABS: If this light appears on your dashboard it means there is a fault somewhere in your anti-locking brake system and should be checked by a mechanic as soon as possible.

These are just some of the common symbols on your dashboard. Your car manufacturer may have some more symbols which communicate problems in the car to you.

BEFORE YOU OPEN YOUR BONNET:

1. All under bonnet checks should be done when the engine is turned off.
2. If the engine has been running for any length of time it is likely there will be areas that are very hot!
3. Read your **owner's manual** safety warnings to see if there are any particular safety stickers you should keep an eye out for.
4. If the engine is running, don't put your hands near any fans or belts.

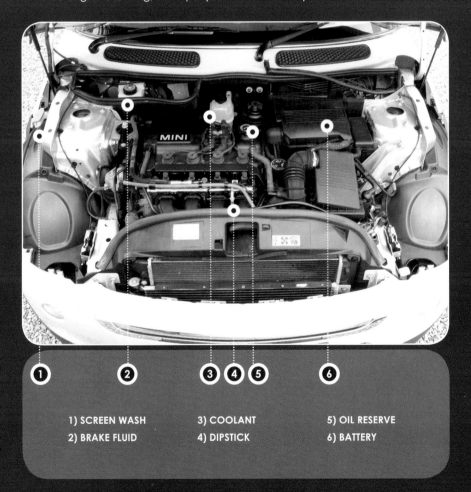

1) SCREEN WASH   3) COOLANT   5) OIL RESERVE

2) BRAKE FLUID   4) DIPSTICK   6) BATTERY

CHECKING YOUR OIL

You should check the oil of your car about every two weeks.

Your car should be stationary for at least five minutes before checking your oil so you can get an accurate oil reading.

A. Locate your dipstick

B. Remove the dipstick

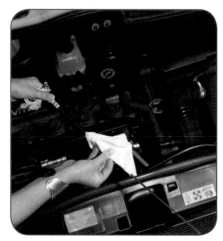

C. Clean it with a rag or paper towel

D. Put the dipstick back in fully for about 5 seconds

E. **Remove the dipstick again slowly**

F. **If the oil level falls below the min mark you need to refill**

You refill the oil via the oil reserve tank. It usually has a picture of an oil canister on it but if you are unsure of where it is; consult your **owner's manual.**

There are two different types of oil for cars – synthetic and non-synthetic. Again, consult your **owner's manual** to see what type your car takes. Most petrol stations and garages will stock both types.

Just because you buy a whole container full of oil doesn't mean you have to put it all in. Stop every now and then when you are refilling and check your oil levels again to make sure you haven't passed the full mark.

COOLANT/ANTI-FREEZE

The cooling system of the car is under high pressure and contains fluid that can heat to a higher temperature than water. Therefore, never open or go near the coolant reserve tank or radiator of a car that has just been running.

 Check your **owner's manual** to find out where your coolant reserve tank is located.

It is usually translucent white so you can inspect the fluid levels without opening it. Be careful not to confuse it with the windshield washer tank, as they look similar.

The reserve tank will have marks on the side of it with "full-hot" or "full-cold" (remember from science class that when things are hot they expand and when they are cold they contract – hence there are two levels). If your level is below "full-cold" when your engine is cold you will need to add fluid until it is near that mark.

> If the level continually falls to below "full-cold" after adding fluid you probably have a leak which should be checked as soon as possible.

FULL HOT

FULL COLD

 Check your **owner's manual** to determine the exact fluid you need to add to your cooling system.

BRAKE FLUID

The brake fluid reservoir is under the bonnet, usually in front of the steering wheel.

Most cars today have a transparent reservoir so you can see the level without opening the cover.

Changing brake fluid is something that should be left to the professionals, so in this instance just make sure that the brake fluid levels are above the minimum mark.

If you notice a drop in the levels below the minimum you will need to bring your car into a mechanic as it is an indication that there is a fault somewhere in your braking system.

If the level noticeably drops over a short period of time or goes down to about only two thirds full: have your brakes checked as soon as possible.

SCREEN WASH

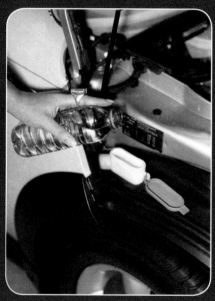

This may not seem very important but if a big truck has ever splashed mud on your screen on a wet day you will know the importance of having screen wash!

Most modern cars will tell you when your screen wash is running low.

You can buy screen wash or a dilution (which you add to water) at your local petrol station.

Don't be tempted to just put water in! It is important to include a screen wash additive as the additive contains anti-freeze which will stop it from freezing in the winter months. It also has cleaning agents which will help clean your windscreen.

TYRE PRESSURE

WHY IS TYRE PRESSURE IMPORTANT?

Driving with a tyre that is substantially under or over-inflated can result in tyre failure. This can be really dangerous if you're driving fast as you can lose control of the car. The wrong tyre pressure can also mean that the breaking capability is dramatically reduced which, if you are driving at speed, can make you lose control.

Having an under-inflated tyre shortens the life of the tyre and means your car has to work harder (which ultimately uses more fuel unnecessarily – more money: less shopping!).

HOW DO I KNOW WHAT MY TYRE PRESSURE IS?

You can find out what tyre pressure your car needs by consulting your **owner's manual.** However, sometimes it is written in the glove compartment, driver's door jamb or inside the petrol cap. Some makes of car require different air pressure in the front tyres compared to the back.

Most petrol stations have a tyre pressure gauge in the service area that you can use.

Note: Tyre pressure needs to be checked when the tyres are cold, so ideally check them after a very short journey (i.e. from your house to your nearest petrol station).

Door jamb

Don't forget to check your spare tyre too. Many a person will tell the sad tale of how they got a flat tyre only to discover their spare had deflated too!

CHECKING YOUR TYRE PRESSURE

- Remove the cap (these can get lost but it should be OK without them).

- Put top of pressure gauge around the seal. **(A)**

- Make sure the gauge completely covers all parts of the seal and no air is escaping (i.e. there is no hissing sound). **(B)**

- Read the pressure levels. **(C)**

- If the reading on the screen is the same as the one your tyres should have then no further action is required on this tyre. Continue to the next tyre and repeat.

- If the pressure reading you are getting is less than the level it is supposed to be at; you need to add more air. To add more air to your tyres increase the pressure gauge to the amount required for your tyre. **(D)**

- Return to your tyre and ensuring that the gauge completely covers the valve the system should add the right amount of air to your tyre. **(E)**

- Once you have finished, replace the cap back on the valve (if you can find it!).

A. Put pressure gauge around seal

B. Ensure gauge completely covers all parts of seal

C. Read pressure levels

D. Increase pressure gauge to amount required

E. Return to your tyre and allow gauge to add air

TYRE CONDITION

You should inspect the condition of your tyres every two weeks, while you are checking the air pressure. Look for any excessive wear, cracks, bulging or deep cuts. If you find any of these on your tyres; they need to be replaced.

You also need to check the tread on the tyre. The tread is the grooved surface on your tyre which helps your tyres grip the ground. If your tread wears down, or becomes bald this can become very dangerous as they won't be able to grip the road properly and you can lose control of your car.

Most countries have laws specifying a minimum tread depth that your tyres must have. It is usually around 1.6mm.

Most new tyres have a built-in tread wear indicator. When the tyres are worn down to this level they need to be replaced.

Tread depth indicator

> **To get the best view for checking the indicator – turn the wheels out.**

THE TREAD ON YOUR TYRES CAN ALSO GIVE YOU AN INDICATION OF THINGS GOING WRONG:

1. If the tread is deeper on the edges than in the centre: the tyre is probably over-inflated.

2. If the tread is deeper in the centre than the edges: the tyre is probably under-inflated.

3. If the tread is deeper on one side than the other: you have to get your wheel alignment checked soon.

4. If the tread is smooth in one direction, but jagged on the other: you have what is called a "saw tooth" wear pattern which is caused by a toe-in problem. A toe-in is when the alignment of the front wheels is closer together than the back.

WINDSCREEN WIPERS

As you use wipers they begin to wear down. They should be changed once or twice a year, depending on their usage. Some manufacturers recommend every 6,000 to 10,000 miles.

You can tell when your wipers are wearing down as they begin to smear the glass or make noise when they're in use.

1. Depending on your wiper blade you will either have to pull or push your wiper from the main body to remove it.

You can purchase windscreen wipers from most petrol stations or you can go to a motor factor shop. You can also go to your car's dealer centre and purchase the manufacturer's recommended wipers – although those will probably be more expensive.

You can replace the whole wiper blade or just replace the rubber insert which is slightly more tricky.

2. Insert the new wiper. You generally will hear a click as it goes into place.

3. Replace wiper to windscreen.

WHEEL ALIGNMENT

Wheel alignment and wheel balancing are two totally different things but people often get them confused.

Wheel alignment means adjusting the angles of the wheels so they are perpendicular to the ground and parallel with each other. Aligning your wheels maximises the life length of the tyres.

SIGNS YOUR WHEELS ARE OUT OF ALIGNMENT:

1. Uneven or rapid tyre wear.
2. Pulling or drifting when you are driving in a straight line.
3. The spokes of your steering wheel are off to one side when you are driving on a straight road.

If you are experiencing any of these problems you need to bring your car to a mechanic or a tyre centre to get your wheels aligned.

WHEEL BALANCING

If you experience vibrations from your steering wheel (or in the seat or floorboard) when you are driving at high speeds it is likely that you need to get your wheels balanced. This is another operation that needs to be carried out by the professionals. You can bring your car to your friendly local mechanic or tyre centre.

BODY WORK

Scratches and scrapes are all part of the driving process. Some people scratch and scrape more than others, but if you leave a scratch untreated rust can set in. This destroys the metal underneath and you will have to get the whole panel replaced. This is pricey!

Replacing the entire section will probably leave you out of pocket even more when you try and resell the car. Scrapes and scratches reduce the resale price of the car. Re-spraying parts can be expensive but it's worth it.

When you are having your car sprayed don't be afraid to call several places to get a quote. You may find that the quotes vary greatly and you might get yourself a great deal!

SPOTTING PROBLEMS

A FEW THINGS TO LOOK OUT FOR...

Watch out for leaks or stains under the car. If you notice your car is leaving any patches of fluid on the ground it is likely you have a leak and need to bring your car to a mechanic.

If you are constantly having to replace a fluid (e.g. oil) this means you could have a leak.

Be aware of any of your controls when you are driving and if anything feels a little unusual make a note of it and inform your mechanic. For example: Stiff gear change; an unusual sensation in your pedal; your steering feels different or you hear strange noises.

CAR SERVICE

In order to get the very best from your car you need to look after it and make sure it has regular check-ups. This means taking it to the garage for a service. Unfortunately for your pocket, all cars need to be regularly serviced. Check your **owner's manual** to find out how often you should bring your car into the mechanic for a service. Don't try and avoid it! Remember, continually paying small amounts for on-going service will mean you won't have to pay out huge whopping sums that you can't afford when major things go wrong. Think of it like investing in good skin care products – pay the little extra now and you'll avoid the hugely expensive repair work later on!

VISITING YOUR LOCAL FRIENDLY MECHANIC

It's safe to say that most girls dread a trip to the mechanic. You nervously hand over your car, wracking your brains trying to remember the last time you had it serviced. You return a few days later only to be told that this and that are wrong with it, most of which you don't understand. Then you hand over all your money and say goodbye to that two weeks in Spain with the girls. Then, there's that niggling suspicion that, could it be, that Mr. Local Friendly Mechanic is taking advantage of the fact that you're FEMALE?!

HERE ARE A FEW TIPS TO TRY AND MINIMISE THE EMOTIONAL TRAUMA:

1. Go in sounding knowledgeable. Use this book to help you determine what's wrong with your car so you can tell him what the problem is (not the other way round). If possible use some mechanical terminology to convince him.

2. Get recommendations. Ask friends to recommend a reliable and trustworthy mechanic.

3. Make sure they are qualified – don't be tempted to give your car to a mate's brother who'll do it for less.

Section 3
WHEN THINGS GO WRONG

4. If you need a lot of work done don't be afraid to haggle or call several other garages to get a comparison quote.

5. Agree the work (and price) you want the mechanic to do. Sometimes when they start working on the car they find other things wrong with it. Tell the mechanic to call you before he carries out any other additional work that will increase your bill when you collect your car.

6. The purpose of this book is to empower girls when it comes to their car. However, as a last resort, if you don't think you will be able to talk the talk in this situation then it might be a good idea to bring your trusty "I know all about cars" male (or female) friend with you to do the talking on your behalf. It's good to make them feel useful!

WHO DO I GO TO?

Repairing cars has become a very specialised service so when something goes wrong with your car make sure you contact the right person.

Crash repairs: repair any damage done to the exterior of your car (also known as panel beater).

Mechanic: carry out all work involving your engine.

Tyre centre: sell tyres and perform wheel alignment and balancing.

Auto-electrician: fixes any electrical problems (e.g. alarms, problems with your battery or lights).

Car dealership: Even if you didn't buy your car from an authorised dealership, occasionally when something goes wrong you will have to deal with a certified dealership for your make of car. You can find your nearest dealership by looking up your car make in the phonebook. You will need to go to a dealership if you lose your car keys; have problems with your alarm or need to buy a specialised part for your car. Car dealerships can also carry out servicing, but they tend to be more expensive compared to other mechanics.

FLAT TYRE

So, you are driving along, and your car begins to feel a bit bumpy and the steering starts to pull to one side – the chances are you have a flat tyre. Decide on a suitable expletive, swear loudly and pull in to the side of the road as soon as it's safe!

Changing a flat tyre seems to be the thing about cars that girls are scared of the most but it's really quite simple. You should have a **jack** in your car which does all the heavy lifting for you. The only heavy lifting you have to do is lifting the tyre itself. Believe it or not it should take you less than 15 minutes – which is quicker than waiting for someone to come and save you!

> **Warning – your hands are going to get dirty!**

WHAT YOU NEED:

1. **A safety triangle**
2. **A jack**
3. **A wheel brace**
4. **Nut tightener**

1. Safety always comes first so make sure your hand brake is on. If you have a safety triangle place it about 10m behind the car to notify other drivers.

2. If your car has a chock – a piece of metal which you place under the front wheel to stop your car rolling – use it.

3. Prepare yourself. Set out your owner's manual, spare tyre, jack and wheel brace within the vicinity of the flat tyre. If you have a wheel cover you must lever this away from the tyre first.

4. Loosen the bolts on the tyre by revolving them about half a revolution in an anti-clockwise direction with the wheel brace. Don't be afraid to use your legs if they are very stiff! But don't remove them fully yet.

Usually, you need to turn the nuts anti-clockwise to loosen and clockwise to tighten

If you have alloys you may need to remove a special bolt. Consult your **owner's manual** and follow the instructions for removing alloys.

5. Next you need to locate the "jacking point" on the car. This is a reinforced bit on the underside of your car which you place your jack under. This will take the weight of the car when the jack is raising it up without damaging the undercarriage of your car.

You can look or feel to find the jacking point. Alternatively consult your owner's manual which should tell you where it is located.

You need to use the jacking point which is closest to the tyre you are changing.

6. Place the jack on the ground underneath the jacking point.

7. Turn the jack in a clockwise direction.

8. Keep turning the jack until the tyre you are changing is lifted a few inches off the ground.

9. Using your fingers, the wheel brace or nut key; unscrew the nuts fully.

10. When all the nuts have been removed, lift the wheel away from the car.

11. Replace the old tyre with the spare. Warning – It can be quite tricky to align the holes in the tyres with the studs!

12. Fasten the nuts in place as tight as you can with your fingers.

13. Lower the jack. When the car has been lowered to its normal level, fully tighten the nuts with your foot until the wheel brace can not turn any more.

Note: If you have a space saver tyre, it is only meant to be for temporary use – enough to bring you to a garage or tyre centre. Do not treat this as a normal tyre.

FLAT BATTERY

Always take care when handling batteries as they contain toxic chemicals and incorrect handling can cause serious injuries. Keep children and naked flames away from the battery.

If you turn your ignition key and all you hear is a constant clicking or tapping noise it means you are having problems with your battery.

The first thing to do is to check that your battery isn't covered in dirt. If it is dirty; clean the points on the battery as this might help the problem.

If you do this and it still doesn't work then this means your battery is dead and you will have to **jump-start** the car. But not to worry, it's really quick and easy, once you know how.

A. You will need to find a kind person who has a car with a fully charged battery and a good pair of jump leads.

B. Position the "working" car so it is front to front with the "flat" car. If it is not possible to line the cars in this way, line them up so the batteries are close together and the jump leads can reach from one battery to the other.

C. Make sure both cars are positioned in neutral.

D. Make sure the radio and the lights on the "flat" car are switched off.

Place cars bumper to bumper.

E. Your battery may have a cover over it. If it does – remove it.

F. Attach the red lead of the jump leads to the positive point on the flat car's battery. Usually, the positive point is either red in colour or has a "plus" sign on it.

G. Attach the other end of the red lead to the positive point of the working car.

H. Attach the black lead of the jump leads to the negative point on the flat car's battery. The negative point is usually black in colour and has a "minus" sign on it.

I. Attach the other end of the black lead to the negative point of the working car's battery.

J. Let the working car start up and rev its engine (in neutral) for about 20 seconds.

K. After this time turn on the ignition of the flat car and it should turn on for you.

L. If the flat car's engine begins to work, rev its engine (in neutral) and keep it running for a while to recharge the battery.

Batteries only have a limited life span – on average 3.5 years. After this, once a battery starts to fail it very rarely responds to recharging and you will need to replace it.

M. Now, carefully remove the jump leads attached from both engines.

N. It is best if you drive the formally flat car around or leave the engine running in neutral for a while so it can recharge itself.

Note: Just because your battery is flat doesn't necessarily mean it is "dead" though. It may just mean that you have been doing lots of short trips or have left it dormant and it hasn't had a chance to recharge itself.

If you're still having constant battery problems but you are sure that there is nothing wrong with your battery then you could have an alternator fault. Dim headlights can be a sign of this. Seek advice from your mechanic.

LOST KEYS

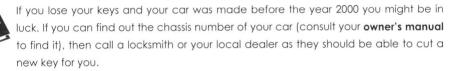

If you lose your keys and your car was made before the year 2000 you might be in luck. If you can find out the chassis number of your car (consult your **owner's manual** to find it), then call a locksmith or your local dealer as they should be able to cut a new key for you.

However, if your car was made after the year 2000 it is more than likely that losing your key is going to turn into an expensive and troublesome experience! Most car keys made after 2000 have a special microchip (called a **transponder**) in the body of the key.

When you put your key into the ignition there is a device which reads the microchip and will only allow the key to turn if it has this special microchip in it. So, if you lose your keys you are going to have to get a new key with a microchip. Locksmiths do not have the capability to programme these microchips, so you must get it programmed at a car dealership.

WHAT TO DO NEXT:

1. Unless your local dealership has a service where they can come to you, you will have to get your car towed to your nearest car dealership – expense number one.

2. They will cut the key for you – expense number two.

3. Then they will programme the key for you – expense number three.

4. Note that car dealerships are only open during normal working hours so if you lose your keys outside of these hours, there is nothing you can do until they re-open.

Now that you can appreciate how troublesome and expensive losing a key is, try to make sure you keep your spare set of keys somewhere safe. Replacing a lost key nowadays will dig into your holiday fund!

FAULTY ALARM

Occasionally, it can happen that your alarm will go off for no reason. This suggests that you have a fault in your alarm system. It will siren for 4 or 5 hours before it flattens the battery and dies. By then you'll have a grumpy neighbour AND a flat car battery to add to your woes!

It is unlikely your mechanic will be able to solve the problem. If your alarm is faulty you will have to get this repaired by an auto-electrician or your car dealership.

Section 4
CAR DOCTOR

Car Doctor...

QUESTIONS AND ANSWERS

Q. When I try to start my car my engine won't start but there is a clicking noise. What causes this?

A. It sounds like your battery is flat! Turn to page "45" to find out how to recharge this. If your battery is more than 3.5 years old it may need to be replaced.

Q. I have tried starting my car but it won't start. However, the headlights are working full beam. What do you recommend?

A. It sounds like it could be more of an ignition problem than a battery problem so jump-starting the battery might not help. You will need to call a mechanic.

Q. I'm driving my car normally but it feels like there is a lot less power. Could you help?

A You probably have faulty ignition timing. You will need to bring it to a mechanic to get it checked out.

Q. I noticed droplets of water coming from my exhaust pipe. What do you think is wrong?

A. Oh dear. It sounds like you could have damaged or blown your head gasket. You will need to get a mechanic to check it out. Don't drive your car to them – get them to call out to you. Be warned, if your head gasket has blown it is not going to be cheap!

Q. Sometimes when I have been sitting in traffic for a while, a cloud of blue smoke comes out of my exhaust. What could that be?

A. This could mean one of your cylinder heads needs replacing. You will need to bring it to your mechanic to get it checked out.

Q. When I put my foot on the brake pedal I feel a pulsating/vibrating sensation. Can you explain?

A. It is most likely that your brake discs are damaged which will need to be repaired by a mechanic.

Q. The lights in my car are constantly blowing and needing to be replaced. Why is that?

A. It could be that your alternator voltage is set too high. Perhaps a job for the auto-electrician.

Q. I can hear a heavy knocking noise coming from my engine when I am driving?

A. It could be that the bearings in your engine are worn or need to be replaced. Your mechanic should be able to deal with this.

Q. I can hear a hissing noise coming from my engine when I am driving. What is that?

A. It sounds like you have a leak in your intake manifold. If this is the case, you will need to get your gasket tightened or replaced by a mechanic.

Section 5
YOUR CAR & THE ENVIRONMENT

Ok girls, let's face it, we love our cars but we also love our home - planet earth! You would have to be living under a rock not to know that the CO_2 emissions from cars are contributing to global warming. If you want to know how you can help here are some handy tips:

HOW CAN I HELP?

Choose a car with the lowest CO_2

Environmentally conscious people can compare cars by the grammes of CO_2 they produce per kilometre. The lower the grammes of CO_2 emissions the better. Check out a website such as **www.carpages.co.uk/co2/** to find out how your car compares. Fuel efficient cars are cheaper to run so will be kinder on your pocket too.

Do you really need to use your car this time?

It can be hard to function in today's society without a car but a lot of us can get into the habit of becoming too dependent on our cars and you might have noticed your waistline expanding too! Try to cut out using your car for any trips under 2km. Walk or cycle instead. If there is a public transport system that can get you to your destination, why don't you leave the car at home and use that instead? Let someone else negotiate the traffic and parking for you!

Car pool

Is there someone you can share a lift to work with? Car pooling is a great way of reducing the amount of cars unnecessarily on the road and a great way of catching up on the gossip too!

Keep your car tuned

If you keep your car properly tuned by having it regularly serviced you can save yourself several full tanks of petrol every year. Under-inflated tyres make your car work harder and use up to 10% more petrol, so check your tyre pressure regularly.

INDEX

A

abs	20
accelerator	7
air filter	7
alternator	11, 20, 50, 57
anti-freeze	24, 26
auto-electrician	35
axels	9

B

battery	7, 11, 15, 20, 21, 35, 45-50, 56
bearings	10, 57
body work	33
bonnet	15, 19
brake fluid	14, 20-21, 25
brake fluid reservoir	21, 25
brake pads	14
brakes	14, 20, 57

C

caliper	14
camshaft	7-8 , 10, 12
car dealership	21, 35
car pool	61
catalytic converter	12
chassis number	51
chock	40
CO_2	61
compression	5

compression stroke	5
coolant	13, 21, 24
cooling system	12, 24
crankshaft	5, 7-10, 12
crash repairs	35
cylinder	3, 4-8, 11, 13, 15, 57
cylinder bank	6
cylinder head	13, 57

D

dashboard symbols	20
dipstick	21-23
disc brakes	14, 57
distributor	8, 11
door jamb	27
drum brakes	14

E

ecu	10
electronic control unit	10
engine block	13
environment	61
exhaust system	12
exhaust valve	4, 5, 12

F

flat battery	45-50
flat tyre	39-44
Four-stroke-combustion-cycle	4, 5

G

H

I

J

K

L

M

mechanic	34-35

N

non-synthetic oil	23
nut tightener	39

O

oil	10, 13, 19-23
oil pan	10
oil reserve	21, 23
output shaft	9
owner's manual	19

P

panel beater	35
piston	4-5, 7-8, 10
pressure gauge	27

R

radiator	12, 15, 24
regulator	11
re-spraying	33
rev counter	6
revs	6
revs per minute	6
rotor	14

S

safety triangle	39
screen wash	21, 26
service	34-35
space saver	44
spark plug	4-5, 8, 11, 15
starter motor	7
sump	10
synthetic oil	23

T

timing belt	8, 12
torque	5
transmission	8-9
transponder	51
tread	30
tread depth	30
tread depth indicator	30
turbo boost	7
turbo charged	7
tyre centre	32, 35
tyre condition	30
tyre pressure	26-29, 61

W

water pump	12
wheel alignment	30, 32, 35
wheel balancing	32
wheel brace	39
windscreen wipers	31

Thank you

We have to say a big thank you to Dermott Lee for
helping us put this book together.

He is a wonderful mechanic and body work specialist who
was responsible for re-spraying the car in this book pink!

If you need a mechanic or body work done call:
Dermott Lee on (01) 4013683 or you can call into him directly at
Q10 Greenogue Business Park, Rathcoole, Co. Dublin.